TODAY'S STREET DANCE

by Lori Mortensen

CAPSTONE PRESS
a capstone imprint

Snap is published by Capstone Press,
1710 Roe Crest Drive, North Mankato, Minnesota, 56003.
www.mycapstone.com

Library of Congress Cataloging-in-Publication Data is available
on the Library of Congress website.
ISBN: 978-1-5435-5445-8 (library hardcover) — 978-1-5435-5449-6 (eBook PDF)

Summary: Explore the hottest trends, current dancers, and most electrifying moves
of today's street dance.

Editorial Credits
Gena Chester, editor; Kay Fraser, designer; Morgan Walters, media researcher;
Tori Abraham, production specialist

Photo Credits
Getty Images: Earl Gibson III, bottom 27, Ethan Miller, 23, FOX, top 27, MARCO LONGARI, 9,
Mat Hayward, top 15, NBC, bottom 15, bottom 29, Sean M. Haffey, bottom 21; Newscom: Alberto
E. Tamargo/Sipa USA, 5, PictureGroup/Sipa USA, top 21, Sthanlee B. Mirador_Pacific Rim, 24;
Shutterstock: Antonio Scorza, 17, chaoss, Cover, chaoss, top 7, DavidTB, bottom 7, Grisha Bruev,
19, Jose Gil, 11, Kiselev Andrey Valerevich, 13, Oleksandr Nagaiets, 22, SFROLOV, 25, Yerchak
Uladzimir, 16

Printed in the United States of America.
001360

Table of Contents

CHAPTER 1

On Top of the World

A spotlight shines down on two tall men. They're dressed in red. In a flash, drumbeats pound. Their heads jerk to the rhythm and unleash a surprising blend of hard-hitting moves. It's an exciting bag of dance tricks they call "crazy stuff." Unlike some dancing duos, these men have a unique presence. It commands the audience's attention. They weave an amazing story through their jaw-dropping **choreography.**

They are Larry and Laurent Nicolas Bourgeois, identical twins, from Paris, France.

When Larry and Laurent Nicolas Bourgeois, known as Les Twins, won NBC's 2017 *World of Dance* competition, the crowd roared. Confetti cannons exploded. Les Twins were on top of the world. They were the new face of street dancing. Their original moves blazed the way in an art form that continues to change, evolve, and transform.

choreography—the arrangement of steps, movements, and required elements that make up a routine

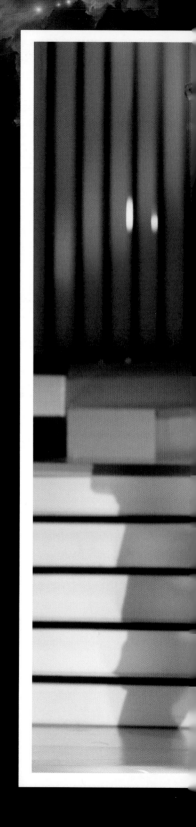

Fact

Les Twins began dancing when they were young. They didn't have formal training but learned by watching other performers. Their street style is sometimes called Twins-Style.

CHAPTER 2

Dancing in the Streets

Street dancing is a wide-ranging style of dance that evolved outside of traditional studios. Street dancers use hip-hop, break dancing, funk, and many more styles to snag audiences. It began in New York in the 1970s. While African-American **DJs** played funk and soul music, crowds danced at block parties. Dancers borrowed moves from popular culture and from each other. Moves from tap, martial art films, and the moves of soul singer, James Brown were all included.

Then, DJ Kool Herc came up with an idea. If he played a song using two turntables, the rhythmic "break" could last twice as long. Kids who danced during the break were called "break" dancers. Herc called them b-boys and b-girls.

DJs "rapping" and "scratching" while music played added to the new sound. This inspired dancers to come up with new moves. As they danced, competitions heated up in one-on-one dance battles. Later, kids competed as dance crews. To win, dancers needed bigger and better moves. Headstands, head spins, leg sweeps, and **acrobatics** were crowd favorites. Break dancing was the first style of dance that became known as street dancing.

DJ—Disc Jockey; DJs play pre-recorded music for a radio, party, or club audience
acrobatics—movements borrowed from gymnastics, such as handstands, flips, and forward rolls

pike freeze

backhand spring

Fact

Hip-hop and street dance are often confused as the same thing. But while street dancers use elements of hip-hop in their choreography, they're also influenced by jazz, contemporary, and many more styles.

A Movement

Today, street dance can be used in a variety of ways—even as a form of protest. Members of Black Lives Matter looked for different ways to communicate their message. Their search led them to Leimert Park in Los Angeles. There, Shamell Bell created a movement she named "street dance **activism**."

Bell eventually put together a crew called The Balance Collective. The group of L.A. artists and dancers create pieces that address social issues.

With the efforts of people like Bell, street dance activism is here to stay. Groups have performed in front of politicians' homes, police headquarters, and on college campuses. Through street dance, young people's voices are being heard.

activism—action that works for social or political change

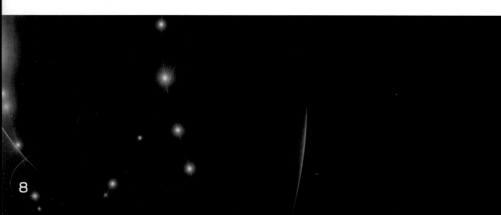

Protesters dance in Johannesburg, South Africa.

MAEDEH HOJABRI

Dance activism isn't just limited to the United States. Around the world, people post videos to social media sites to draw attention to important causes.

In July 2018, women all over the world posted videos of themselves dancing to protest the recent arrest of Maedeh Hojabri. She is an Iranian woman who frequently posted dance videos of herself on Instagram. Unfortunately, dancing in public spaces is illegal in Iran.

Hojabri was arrested and forced to issue an apology on TV. Many people protested Hojabri's arrest and used a hashtag that translates to "dancing isn't a crime" to show their support.

CHAPTER 3

Street Smarts

Before dancers perform, they need the right gear. For street dancing, that means loose clothing. Common attire includes sweat pants or loose-fitting jeans paired with tees, tanks, or jerseys.

Street clothes not only add to a dancer's style, they also allow dancers to move freely. Layers are helpful too. Once dancers warm up, they may ditch some layers to keep cool. The final touch? Some comfy tennis shoes. The right shoes offer the perfect blend of traction, comfort, and movement.

Fact

France's Salah Benlemqawanssa, also known as Spider Salah, is one of the most popular street dancers in the world. He wears hats to give him a style that adds to his unique blend of popping, animation, and other styles.

A street performer wows the crowd with his break-dancing skills.

Dancers need to warm up before they start a performance. They put on some music and start with small movements. As dancers get going, they add a bounce to their step. Then, they might add some shoulder rolls. Stretching their arms, legs, neck, and torso will get their body loose and ready to move.

Once dancers are warmed up, they're ready to tackle bigger moves. If they try and hit power moves without warming up, they might get injured. An injury can hold dancers up for weeks.

Dancing is demanding. It takes a lot out of dancers' bodies and requires them to use a lot of energy. To maintain their health, they need a balanced diet. It's important for dancers to eat breakfast and small meals throughout the day. Their diet should also include **protein** and **carbohydrates.**

Street dancers practice and learn moves many different ways. One way to learn is to pick up steps from friends. Another is watching videos on YouTube. Taking a class in an unfamiliar style of dance is another great option. Taking dance classes on a regular basis builds stamina, strength, and discipline. Dancers benefit by putting it all out there and getting feedback from professionals.

protein—a substance found in foods such as meat, cheese, eggs, and fish that helps build muscle
carbohydrates—a substance found in foods such as bread, rice, cereal, and potatoes that gives you energy

Fact

One of the hardest power moves is the jackhammer. While the dancer is spread out on the floor, supported by one hand, he or she spins around by hopping, balancing, and turning on that hand.

CHAPTER 4

Moves to Know

The beauty of street dance is that there are no rules. But that doesn't mean dancers come unprepared. A majority of street dancers study and develop moves for their performance.

Pop and Lock

Popping and **locking** aren't just steps. They're two different styles that go together like Kool Herc's turntables. Popping is all about muscle contractions and isolations. When dancers pop, it looks like they've been zapped with a charge of electricity. That's where the isolations come in. Dancers contract their muscles in certain places like their arms, legs, or head. This creates that sudden, surprising twitch. Boogaloo Sam invented this highly charged move in the late 1970s. One of the most popular poppers today is Poppin' John. He amazes crowds everywhere with his sharp, electric moves.

Dancers often combine popping with locking. Locking is all about freezing—as if the dancer is suddenly locked in place. Don "Campbelllock" Campbell, who performed with the Lockers, invented this move in 1970. This style also involves isolations. Today, Dushaunt Stegall, or Fik-Shun, is well-known for his pop-and-lock skills. He was the winner of *So You Think You Can Dance* in 2013.

popping—contracting nad relaxing muscles to make short, quick, and explosive movements
locking—freezing in a certain position after a fast movement

One of the hottest dance crews today is Just Jerk. Americans got their first look at this crew when they performed on *America's Got Talent* in 2017. Dressed in shiny red outfits, this South Korean crew thrilled audiences with their complex, high-energy performance.

Street performers dancing in front of a crowd in New York City.

Body Waves

Another street dance style? Body waves. Unlike the sharp movements of popping and locking, body waves ripple through the dancer's body from one place to another.

It looks as if there's an invisible ball of energy moving inside. Head to toe, arm to arm, dancers can send the ripple anywhere—even to someone else!

The Worm

A favorite move is The Worm. Dancers start in a push-up position, flat on the floor, with their elbows bent. By quickly kicking their legs up and back, they get the first **undulation** started as their head and torso come up. As they go, their body starts waving like a worm across the dance floor.

undulation—a wave-like, up-and-down movement

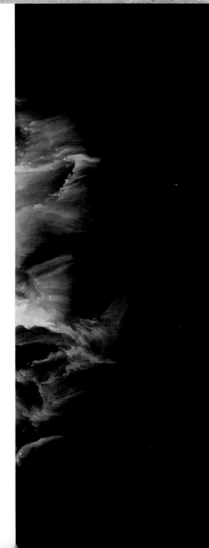

Justin Timberlake performing in Brazil in 2017.

JUSTIN TIMBERLAKE

Justin Timberlake is not only a talented singer, songwriter, and actor. He's also a talented dancer with razor sharp hip-hop skills. Timberlake, together with his accomplished group of backup dancers, dazzle audiences around the world. A recent music video of his showcased a robot dancing.

Tutting

Tutting is another street dance style. The style gets its name from art found in ancient Egypt. Just like the art from that period, tutting is all about angles. Dancers tut by copying right angles and geometric shapes with different parts of their bodies. It's a complex style with countless combinations.

Fact

Finger tutting is a street dance specialty where dancers make complex, geometric shapes with their hands. One of the best finger tutters is John Hunt. He's popularly known as the "King of Fingers."

Airwalking

Airwalking is another fun and challenging dance step. Much like moonwalking, it's all about the illusion. Dancers start by taking a step forward. But instead of putting weight on it, the leg comes back into place. The foot glides through the air, not against the ground. As the dancer alternates legs, it looks as if they're walking on air.

Freestyling

Freestyling is a form of dance where there's no plan at all. It's a chance for dancers to express their creativity through movement. Dancers don't have to follow a choreographer. Instead, they have complete control over what they'll do and the movements they'll invent. Since freestyling is all about originality, no two dances are the same. Dancers use freestyling to show people who they are.

Freestyling still requires practice. Most dancers need to perfect their moves before showing them off to a crowd.

CHAPTER 5

Dance On!

Great dance performances last a lifetime. And even though street dancers don't always plan the exact steps they'll do, they can learn a lot from current performers. Bruno Mars and Beyoncé are great examples to watch. Bruno Mars' smooth moves are eye-catching. Beyoncé's choreography, combined with her chart-topping songs, get people on their feet. Their performances stick in people's minds for a reason. They checked off all the right performance boxes.

Music

In street dance, music often drives the performance. The right music will not only inspire great, innovative movement, it will also get the crowd excited with the first note.

Choreography

Once the music is selected, it's all about the choreography. Exceptional choreography has its own set of boxes. Variety. Intensity. Timing—fast, slow, and freezes. Sometimes stopping the motion makes the most impact. The number of dancers also makes a difference. Will there be a lot, or only one or two? How will the dancers work together? Is there a story between them? Will there be lifts? Changing levels switches things up too. Dancers may jump in the air or stretch out flat on the floor.

Bruno Mars (center) performing at the Grammy Awards in 2018.

Beyoncé and Bruno Mars performing at the Super Bowl 50 half-time show in 2016.

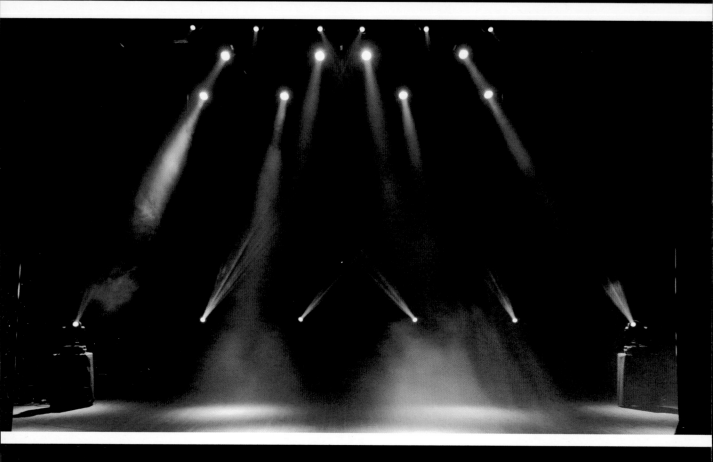

Stage Presence

For street dancers, any space counts as their stage. Standing in one place is **static** and boring. Dancers ramp up the choreography by using all of the stage. Charging forward creates power. Dancers coming in from the sides add surprise and variety. Retreating dancers pull back the energy. R3D Zone's 2018 performance at World of Dance took full advantage of these types of stage dynamics. All the great performances do.

static—lacking in movement

Fact
Jabbawockeez are street dance standouts. They won *America's Best Dance Crew* in 2008. Now, they perform at MGM in Las Vegas.

Story

Great performances don't rely on steps alone. Choreographers use movement to express a story or idea. Fantastic steps are fine. But the most memorable performances add that extra layer to connect with the audience's emotions.

Costumes

Costumes make a visual impact as well. What a dancer wears adds to the performance. Costumes create identity, time, place, and story. For the hip-hop group Jabbawockeez, their stark-white masks give them an unmistakable look that unifies their appearance and performance. Whatever is chosen says something about the dance.

KYLE HANAGAMI

Kyle Hanagami is making his mark in the dance world. Born in Los Angeles, he's an award-winning dancer, teacher, and Internet sensation. Hanagami captures audiences with his unique blend of hip-hop and street jazz. He believes a performance should be for the audience, as much as it is for the choreographer, dancer, or director. In 2017, Hanagami joined *World of Dance* as a supervising choreographer.

Lighting

Lighting is often overlooked, but it's part of the performance package. Lighting creates focus, direction, drama, and mood—from a single spotlight, to a stage lit up like fireworks.

Rehearsals

Unless dancers are freestyling, rehearsing routines pins it all down. While dancing without choreography can create exceptional movements, jaw-dropping performances take time and practice.

CHAPTER 6

Street Dance Sensations

Street dances can happen in any city around the world. It's local, and it's always evolving. Talented street dancers can be found everywhere. But unless they're discovered on social media or through a dance competition, their success usually stays local. There are a few, however, that have achieved worldwide fame.

Better Together

A couple takes center stage. He's wearing a red hat. She's wearing a polka-dotted blouse. They step together and start dancing. But in the story they weave, things start to go wrong. She bumps into him. She apologizes. They start again. Another mistake. The audience starts to feel sorry for this poor, clumsy couple. Then everything changes. They unleash their unbelievable moves. It is another extraordinary performance by Keone and Mari Madrid. A fascinating blend of sweet, lyrical style and hip-hop they call "Urban Dance."

It's not just about dance—it's about the story. A story they skillfully weave into their choreography to draw the audience into their work. When they end at the same place they began, face to face, the crowd at the 2017 *World of Dance* cheers.

Dancers Robert Roldan and Taylor Sieve perform a hip-hop routine choreographed by Keone and Mari Madrid.

Fact

Dancers and choreographers Keone and Mari Madrid dance together and are married to each other. They began dancing in their teens.

Super Human Moves

For Las Vegas' Super Cr3w, it's all about big, **synchronized** moves. That means their entire 11-member crew is doing the same thing at the same time. Dancing in sync is hard to achieve, especially with large numbers. When it happens, it makes a powerful, lasting impression. They couple their style with surprising innovation. For example, they don't do a single leap over one's leg. Instead, it's an entire rotation that whirls the dancer in an air flare. The audience gasps. It looks as if it's a special effect from a martial arts movie. Bam!

Kinjaz, an Asian-American crew based in Los Angeles, blends street dance, Asian culture, and storytelling. Elements of their culture appear in their costumes and set designs, such as sliding Japanese doors and ninja outfits. Their powerful performances reflect their motto, "Respect all . . . fear none."

These sensational dancers are different. But they have important elements in common. Successful street dancers bring unique style to their performances. They dazzle audiences with compelling stories told through their choreography. Street dance is more than just steps. It's an exciting and innovative art that will continue to evolve.

synchronize— when two or more people perform the same movement at the same time

Kinjaz wowed audiences with their combination of costumes and moves in *World of Dance* season 1.

Glossary

acrobatics (AK-ruh-bat-iks)—movements borrowed from gymnastics, such as handstands, flips, and forward rolls

activism (AK-tuh-viz-uhm)—action that works for social or political change

carbohydrates (kahr-boh-HY-drayt)—a substance found in foods such as bread, rice, cereal, and potatoes that gives you energy

choreography (kor-ee-OG-ruh-fee)—the arrangement of steps, movements, and required elements that make up a routine

DJ (DEE-jay)—Disc Jockey; DJs play pre-recorded music for a radio, party, or club audience

locking (LAHK-ing)—freezing in a certain position after a fast movement

popping (POP-ing)—to make short, quick, and explosive movement

protein (PROH-teen)—a substance found in foods such as meat, cheese, eggs, and fish

static (STAH-tik)—lacking in movement

synchronize (SING-kruh-nized)—when two or more people perform the same movements at the same time

undulation (uhn-dew-LAY-shun)—a flowing, up-and-down movement

Read More

Lanier, Wendy Hinote. *Hip-Hop Dance*. Shall We Dance? Lake Elmo, Minn.: Focus Readers, 2018.

Llanas, Sheila. *The Women of Hip-Hop*. Hip-Hop Insider. Minneapolis, Minn.: Abdo, 2019.

Mattern, Joanne. *Hip-Hop Dance*. Dance Studios. Hallendale, Flo.: Mitchell Lane Publishers, 2019.

Internet Sites

Use Facthound to find Internet sites related to this book.

Visit www.facthound.com.

Just type in 9781543554458 and go!

Index